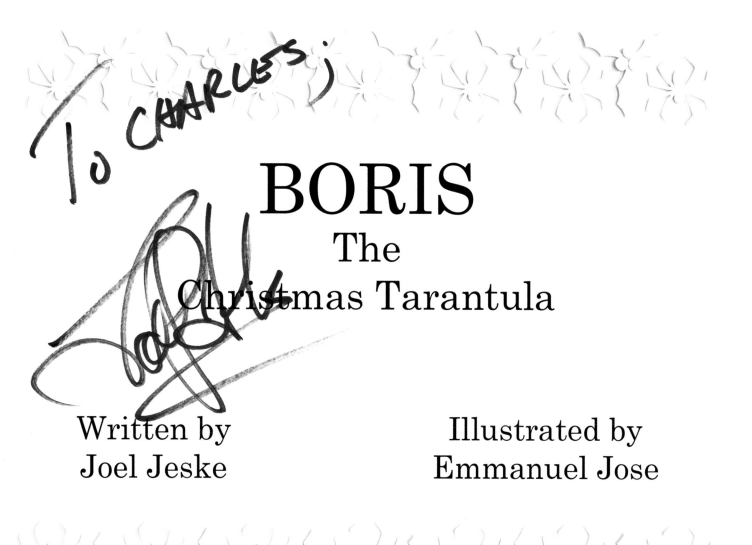

To Charles;

BORIS
The
Christmas Tarantula

Written by
Joel Jeske

Illustrated by
Emmanuel Jose

First edition 2015

ISBN #: 978-1-68222-469-4

The illustrations were cut from paper than then digitally photographed.
For more information about books, the illustrations, or Boris write:
Boris The Christmas Tarantula
370 Fort Washington Ave. #206
New York City, NY 10033

For all of those who believe in the true meaning of Christmas

There once was a tarantula,
Boris, by name,
Who proved tarantulas were not all the same.

He had eight legs and eyes as nature intended.
However, with that,
The similarity ended.

Other spiders were baffled and deeply they feared,
No one would find out what made Boris so weird.

He never went hunting or stalking around.
At tarantula soccer, he would never be found.
He never had seconds of his mom's cricket stew.
He never did anything tarantulas do.

He spent all his time, his heart, and his reason,
In the practice and keeping of one special season.

Boris loved Christmas!
He loved it most of all!
More than his birthday or the Tarantulas' Ball!

He sang Christmas carols while up late at night,
And decorated everything with twinkling light.
He was expert at wrapping and tying all bows!
He knew the true hue of Rudolph's red nose!

He made cookies and cakes, and all Christmas candy!
And being a spider, eight legs were so handy.
For no one could decorate a house just as quick.
No one, of course,
Except good ol' Saint Nick.

"Since my very first Christmas," he would answer quite snappy,
"It's the one thing I know that makes everyone happy!
So, to help all others with sorrow and strife,
I'll celebrate Christmas each day of my life!"

"Please! Give up this notion!" His father did ask.
"It's only one holiday, not a full year round task."

His feelings for Christmas were not understood.
Boris knew he should leave his tarantula "hood."
He'd go to the place where Christmas was made.
And hope that his talents could offer some aid.

November was ending.
He knew he must hurry.
He explained to his parents to stop all their worry.

"You might think I am foolish for what I have vowed."
"Let me follow my dream. I know you will be proud."

Boris left his home burrow when it was first light,
With a hug from his parents, sixteen legs tight.

His travels were long in the world cold and scary.
He was quite afraid,
Though he was big and hairy.
His deep love for Christmas never did waiver,
The toils of his journey made him much braver!
He followed his heart and had faith in his soul,
If he kept walking north, he would reach the North Pole!

After walking for ages, feet frozen in snow,
He simply looked up and…
What do you know?
"Welcome to the North Pole!" a sign brightly read.
Boris had made it!
Now, full steam ahead!

Old Santa was busy with the elves in his shop,
When a knock on the door brought them to a stop.
They opened the door to take a quick peek.
What they saw sitting there made them all shriek!
A giant tarantula was standing therein;
In a hat, gloves, and boots and a big Christmas grin!

"Merry Christmas to all! I'm Boris The Spider!"
He stuck in four legs. The door opened wider.
"I walked thousands of miles to come to help you!
I love Christmas so much! There is much I can do!"

Santa was speechless as Boris drew near.
Most of the elves were all hiding in fear.

"Uh…Thanks," said Santa, "It is most unexpected."
"It is rare that an offer of help is rejected."
"But would not some other place suit you as well."
"Like Halloween? Or Easter? You never can tell."

"Halloween's too scary!" Boris said with a shiver.
"And who wants to work for a painted egg giver?
Please give me a chance. I have much to prove."
Boris smiled at Santa while the elves did not move.

Then quicker than lightning, the spider crawled in,
And jumped up fangs first in an ornament bin.
Before Santa and the elves could cope with their fright,
Boris gave their small workshop a makeover in light.

The Christmas trees glistened!
The décor was inspired!
Santa knew Boris must surely be hired.
The North Pole was delighted!
All gave out a cheer!
But no one came forward, or even got near.

With Christmas so close, there arose an alarm,
That Santa himself could not fix with his charm.
The desire to be good on Christmas was lacking,
With tantrums and fits, spoiled brats were attacking!

They demanded their Christmas with all that they had!
They wanted their presents!
Though they had been bad!
Santa thought, "What in the world can we do?
With no 'naughty and nice', Christmas meaning's not true."

He called an elf council to think really quick.
We need to save Christmas!
Now, whom should they pick?
The choices were dreary.
Some hard for the palate.
Then, Santa saw Boris's name on the ballot.
"The answer is simple! He has fangs and eight feet,
But his passion for Christmas can never be beat!"

So, Boris was called from his dark working place,
And soon found dear Santa an inch from his face.

"I want you to see that the children do good.
And share love for Christmas as all children should!"

"I am ever so honored." Boris said with a tear.
And all of the elves let out an elf cheer!
The problem was solved that all of them cared.
With Boris so busy, they wouldn't be scared.

Boris crawled away quickly.
He went kid to kid.
Making sure it was only good things that they did.

He stopped Sneaky Cecil who wanted to maim.
One look at our Boris, he was never the same.
He gave Roger the Bully an eight-legged hug,
Now Roger is jumpy at the sight of a bug.
He saved Mean Amanda from her screaming and stomping.
With a smile of his fangs, she feared a great chomping.
The brats all went from disrespect to devotion.
For a giant tarantula watched every motion.

"This great news," said Boris, "will make Santa quite glad.
He now knows for Christmas, these children aren't bad."

BEFORE

AFTER

Grandparents were grateful.
The moms and dads raved.
To see all their children so well behaved.

Boris kept bad ideas out of all of their heads,
By showing up nightly at the foot of their beds.
"Always be good!" Boris called out in the night.
"Merry Christmas." said the brats, still frozen with fright.

The reports came in quickly!
The good news was steady!
Santa Claus and the elves were all at the ready!
Boris found the good children,
That much was clear.
Christmas was safe for another great year!

When invited to ride in Santa's great sleigh,
The spider was speechless. What should he say?
With a "YES!" he soon found himself soaring through space.
Working for Christmas, he found his right place.

So, look to the sky on this next Christmas night.
When the moon in the heavens is shining so bright.
You might see a tarantula with a spider smile wide,
And Jolly Saint Nick cowered off to one side.

Please think of this tale as a good thing to hear,
Behave at your best throughout the long year.
And if you desire to cause wreck and ruin,
A spider might ask, "Hey. What are you doin'?"

Be kind to your family and other love givers,
When finding good in ALL children…

Boris always delivers.

THE END